KACEY MUSGRAVES

TWO EXTRAORDINARY PEOPLE.

MAREN MORRIS

CONNECTED LIVES™

Ariana Grande | Camila Cabello

Ed Sheeran | Shawn Mendes

Halsey | Billie Eilish

John Legend | Michael Bublé

Kacey Musgraves | Maren Morris

Kane Brown | Sam Hunt

Kendrick Lamar | Travis Scott

Nicki Minaj | Cardi B

Photo credits: page 4: Noam Galai via Getty Images; page 5: Jason Kempin via Getty Images; page 6: Frederick M. Brown via Getty Images; page 7: Jason Kempin via Getty Images; page 8: Kokoulina via Shutterstock.com; page 10: Rich Fury / Coachella via Getty Images; page 11: Nicholas Hunt / iHeartRadio via Getty Images; page 12: Kevin Winter / The Recording Academy via Getty Images; page 13: Slaven Vlasic via Getty Images; page 16: Jemal Countess / Global Citizen Festival: Mandela 100 via Getty Images; page 17: Michael Loccisano via Getty Images; page 19: Emma McIntyre via Getty Images; page 20: Rick Kern / Samsung via Getty Images; page 21: Rick Diamond via Getty Images; page 22: Rick Diamond via Getty Images; page 23: Cindy Ord / SiriusXM via Getty Images; page 25: Ethan Miller via Getty Images; page 28: Rusty Russell via Getty Images; page 29: Jason Davis / CRS via Getty Images; page 30: Jason Merritt via Getty Images; page 31: Jason Kempin / St. Jude via Getty Images; page 32: Kevork Djansezian via Getty Images; page 33: Rick Diamond / Spotify via Getty Images; page 34: Rick Diamond / 3rd & Lindsley via Getty Images; page 35: Cindy Ord / SiriusXM via Getty Images; page 36: Kevork Djansezian via Getty Images; page 40: Frazer Harrison via Getty Images; page 41: Michael Loccisano via Getty Images; page 42: Christopher Polk / Stagecoach via Getty Images; page 43: Frazer Harrison via Getty Images; page 45: Rick Diamond / CMT via Getty Images; page 47: Rick Kern via Getty Images; page 48: Ethan Miller via Getty Images; page 49: Slaven Vlasic via Getty Images; page 52: Rick Diamond / No Shoes Nation Tour via Getty Images; page 53: Nicholas Hunt / Billboard Magazine via Getty Images; page 55: Rick Diamond via Getty Images; page 56: Rick Diamond via Getty Images; page 58: Ethan Miller via Getty Images; page 59: Kevin Winter / Coachella via Getty Images; page 61: Kevin Winter via Getty Images; page 62: Noam Galai via Getty Images; page 63: Matt Winkelmeyer via Getty Images; page 64: Ethan Miller / Essential Broadcast Media via Getty Images, Matt Winkelmeyer / dcp via Getty Images; background: Chris Wong / EyeEm via Getty Images; Kacey Musgraves head shot: Frazer Harrison via Getty Images; Maren Morris head shot: Frazer Harrison via Getty Images

ISBN: 978-1-68021-796-4
eBook: 978-1-64598-082-7

Printed in Malaysia

24 23 22 21 20   1 2 3 4 5

TABLE OF CONTENTS

CHAPTER 1

EARLY LIFE

WHO IS KACEY MUSGRAVES?

Kacey Musgraves is a country music singer and songwriter. Her birthday is August 21, 1988. She was born in Golden, Texas. This is a small town about 75 miles east of Dallas. Around 200 people live there. Many of them work on farms. Until Kacey became a star, Golden was best known for growing sweet potatoes. Every year there is a festival to celebrate the crop.

WHO IS MAREN MORRIS?

About 100 miles west of Golden is the city of Arlington, Texas. Maren Morris was born there on April 10, 1990. Like Kacey, she became a singer and songwriter. Arlington is much bigger than Golden. It has a population of around 400,000. The big cities of Dallas and Fort Worth are nearby. Other musicians have come from Arlington. Pentatonix, an *a cappella* group, started there.

PRINT SHOP

Kacey's dad, Craig, owns a small printing business. Her mom, Karen, works there too. Karen is also an artist who paints and sculpts. Their shop is near Golden, in the small town of Mineola. Kacey grew up helping around the store. Kelly is her younger sister. She is a photographer. Like Maren, Kacey is the oldest.

COUNTRY SINGERS FROM TEXAS

Over the years, many country music singers have come from Texas. One was Waylon Jennings. Much of his music came out in the 1960s and 1970s. Both Kacey and Maren like his traditional style.

More recent stars are from the Lone Star State too. In 2013, Danielle Bradbery won season four of *The Voice*. Sundance Head was the winner in 2016. The duo Maddie and Tae met in Dallas. Although Tae is from Oklahoma, Maddie is from Sugar Land, Texas.

Sundance Head

HAIR SALON

Maren's parents are Scott and Kellie. Like Kacey's family, they own their own business. It is a hair salon called the Maren Karsen Salon. They named it after Maren and her younger sister, Karsen. Growing up, Maren spent a lot of time helping out at the business. As a teenager, she worked at the salon's front desk.

FORT WORTH STOCK YARDS

THE BUCKAROOS

When Kacey was nine, she and her sister
performed with the Cowtown Opry Buckaroos.
This was a children's singing group. "It was run
by this group of older people that just really loved
country-western music," Kacey told *The Fader.* "They
would mentor younger kids to get out of their shells."
Every weekend, Kacey's parents would drive the
family to Fort Worth. That's where they performed.
All the kids in the group wore red bandanas and
blue jeans.

SINGING KARAOKE

Maren's parents would host parties for their employees. Often, they set up a karaoke machine so everyone could sing. One night, Maren lifted the microphone to her mouth. She started to sing LeAnn Rimes's song "Blue." Her parents were in another room. They thought someone had turned the radio on. Suddenly, they realized it was their daughter. The girl was around nine years old. Singing karaoke at her parents' parties was enjoyable. "I was mostly just goofing around. It was just fun," she told *HuffPost*.

KARAOKE AND COVERS

In the 1970s, the first karaoke machines were made in Japan. These machines play music. People sing along with a microphone. The music is instrumental. This means there are no recorded vocals, just instruments. Usually these are covers of well-known songs. Many singers got their start singing covers of other people's music. Social media lets artists post their music so others can hear. It reaches a wider audience.

WESTERN SWING

Before joining the Buckaroos, Kacey already had experience singing in public. Her interest in music had started at a young age. By the time she was eight, she was already performing. Kacey sang western swing music. These are country classics. Her parents drove her around the state of Texas so she could sing.

TEXAS CIRCUIT

Maren's first experience performing was in Johnnie High's Country Music Revue. This was a long-running weekly variety show in Arlington. It was where many famous singers got their start. "That was my first time being onstage in front of an audience with people behind me, and I think that just changed my life," she told the *Dallas Observer*.

At 11 years old, she started performing around Texas. Like Kacey, this is how she got her start. The two met as teenagers. They often sang at the same places.

"NOTICE ME"

Soon, Kacey wasn't just singing. She was writing music too. Her dad told *Texas Monthly* that she "would listen to whatever we were playing, and then she'd go to her bedroom and write her own songs."

At around nine years old, she wrote "Notice Me." Kacey told CMT News, "I just turned a poem into a song." Another early song was "Movin' On." Her dad explained that the song was "about someone moving off his farm because all the crops had died and there was no water for the cattle."

POETRY

Maren also got an early start with songwriting. Like Kacey, Maren wrote poems first. Later, she got her first guitar. This let her turn those poems into songs.

Growing up, Maren was very shy. Performing helped her gain confidence. "I never remember a time when I wasn't singing," she told YouTube Music. Music helped her to express her creativity. "I was trying to figure out how to get my feelings out."

COUNTRY GIRL

While music took up most of Kacey's time, she still had other interests growing up. As a young girl, she begged her parents to buy her a horse. They didn't. She had to wait until she was an adult for that dream to come true. One interest Kacey's parents did encourage was her love of outer space. Her dad bought a telescope. They looked at the stars together.

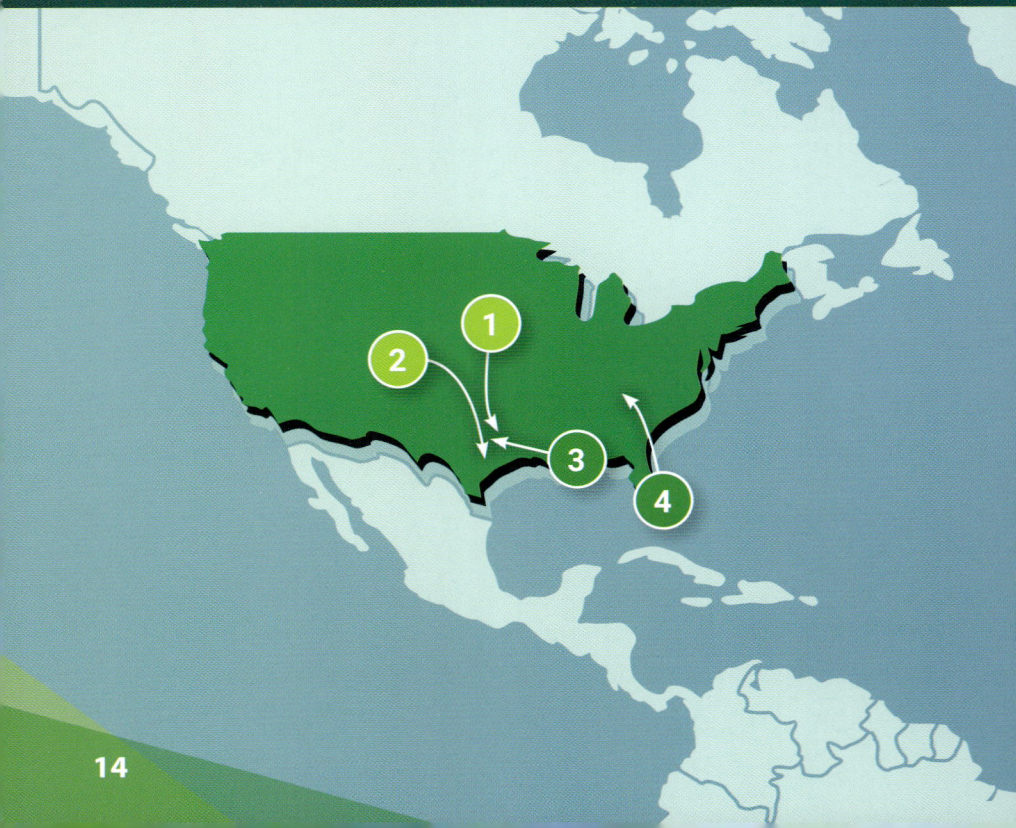

BROADWAY DREAMS

Maren had interests outside of music too. She enjoyed art and painting. In high school, she played soccer. Music took up most of her time, though. As a teenager, Maren was involved in choir and theater. Her goal was to perform on Broadway in New York City. "My dream has always been to play Elphaba in *Wicked*," she told Taste of Country.

KACEY MUSGRAVES

1. **Golden, Texas:** This small town is where Kacey was born.
2. **Austin, Texas:** Kacey moved here after high school. She played gigs around the city, trying to start her career.

MAREN MORRIS

3. **Arlington, Texas:** Maren was born here.
4. **Nashville, Tennessee:** She moved to this city to work as a songwriter.

CHAPTER 2

INTRO TO MUSIC

GUITAR LESSONS

By age 12, Kacey was learning how to play the guitar. She already played the mandolin. Her guitar teacher was John DeFoore. Many of his students had gone on to be successful country musicians. Kacey's teacher challenged her from the beginning. Every week, DeFoore had her write a new song. He wanted her to learn how to write music from the heart.

A GIFT

Maren's father bought the singer her first guitar. She was 12 years old. He taught her how to play a few chords at first. From there, she started to write her own music. "I'd always loved writing in school, I loved creative writing and loved writing poems and short stories. But when I picked up the guitar, it just seemed so natural to put music to lyrics," she told *HuffPost*.

BACKGROUND MUSIC

Kacey's parents had music on constantly in the background at home. They played music by artists like Tom Petty, the Beach Boys, and Sheryl Crow. "I grew up singing western swing and very traditional music, but I also listened to NSYNC or Spice Girls like whatever everybody else was listening to," she told Vice.

MANDOLIN

The mandolin looks like a small guitar, but with a rounder body. Players pluck the strings to produce sounds. Mandolins are used in some country music. It is more common for bluegrass musicians to play the instrument. Bluegrass is similar to country, but with more jazz elements. A mandolin sounds like a higher-pitched guitar. The 2019 song "Pictures" by Judah & the Lion is backed by a mandolin. Kacey also sings on the track.

FAMILY ENCOURAGEMENT

Once Maren's parents realized she could sing, they wanted to encourage her. "I didn't come from a musical family, but I realized I loved to sing," she told Wide Open Country. Like Kacey's family, Maren's listened to country music. They also listened to rock groups like Pink Floyd and Led Zeppelin. "My parents are sort of '60s, '70s kids," Maren explained to *HuffPost*.

TEXAS TWO BITS

In 1999, Kacey formed a duo with another girl her age, Alina Tatum. The two sang in a yodeling style. This is a traditional sound in classic country music. They called themselves the Texas Two Bits.

Two years later, they were invited to perform at an important party. It was for the new president of the United States, George W. Bush. The pair traveled to Washington, D.C., for the event. Other country groups performed too. Kacey was just 12 years old.

DISAPPOINTMENT

At age 14, Maren had an upsetting experience. She performed at a club in Fort Worth. Only two people were in the audience. One was a server who worked there. The other was Maren's dad.

After the show, the club's manager didn't want to pay Maren. It was an eye-opening experience for her. She told *Pacific* magazine how disappointed she was. The singer remembers thinking, "You're really going to take money away from a 14-year-old?"

MOVIN' ON

Kacey's family supported her dream to have a music career. They helped her record an independent album when she was 13. The singer told *The Fader*, "My mom would take my picture for the CD cover." Other family members helped too. "My dad's mom was my booking agent. She'd call places . . . and say, 'Hey, you need to have my granddaughter sing.'" *Movin' On* came out in 2002. Two more independent CDs were recorded after that. *Wanted: One Good Cowboy* came out in 2003. Four years later, *Kacey Musgraves* was released.

WALK ON

Maren also released three albums while growing up. Her first was called *Walk On*. It came out in 2005, when she was 15 years old. Her parents helped her. "We literally sold the furniture out of the house to finance her very first record," Maren's mom told TV station WFAA. Two years later, *All That It Takes* came out. Smith Music Group released the album. Maren had helped write 8 of its 13 songs. This record was followed by *Live Wire* in 2011.

BIG CITY DREAMS

Kacey graduated from high school in 2006. She decided to move to Austin, Texas. Living in a big city would give her more chances than staying in her small hometown. In Austin, the singer looked for opportunities. One job she had there was working for a local booking company. They hired musicians to sing at different places around town. Kacey also auditioned for the TV show *Nashville Star*.

NASHVILLE STAR

Nashville Star was a competitive music show. It aired from 2003 to 2008. Many country music singers were contestants on the show over the years. However, most of the artists who went on to make it big didn't win their seasons. Kacey is one example. Another is Miranda Lambert. She came in third during the first season of the show. Maren tried out but didn't even make it on the show. Singer Chris Young is the most successful person to have won the show. He got first place in 2006.

OFF TO COLLEGE

Maren sang on weekends all through high school. "I was the only kid in school that had a job on the weekends!" she said on her website. After graduating, her next step was going to the University of North Texas. In 2010, she attended for one semester. While there, Maren sang and played keyboard with a band called They Were Stars.

GETTING ON TV

In 2007, Kacey competed on the fifth season of
Nashville Star. This was a country music reality TV
show. The singer was eliminated in the third episode.
She came in seventh place. "I didn't really know what
I was getting myself into," she explained to *The Fader*.
Even though Kacey didn't win, she learned a lot from
the experience. "I was very young and figuring myself
out musically and personally," she told Yahoo! Music.

REALITY SHOW REJECTIONS

In her late teens, Maren auditioned for several reality
shows. She tried out for *American Idol*, *Nashville Star*,
The Voice, and *America's Got Talent*. All of them turned
her down. "I was heartbroken at the time," she told the
Dallas Observer. Maren was getting tired of performing
at shows around Texas. "Eventually, I wanted a new
challenge," she added. It was time for the next step.

PARALLEL LIVES

Plays many instruments

Made it on *Nashville Star*

Born in Texas

Wrote music from a young age

Released three CDs while growing up

Sang in public as a child

Has one younger sister

Plays guitar and a little piano

Rejected from *Nashville Star*, *American Idol*, *The Voice*, and *America's Got Talent*

CHAPTER 3

RISE TO SUCCESS

NASHVILLE

Kacey hadn't made it far on *Nashville Star*. The show did make her realize something, though. Nashville would be good for her career. At age 19, she moved there. Her plan was to work as a songwriter. "When I got to Nashville, I jumped right in. I didn't have a backup plan; I was super fearless," Kacey told *Vanity Fair*. By 2009, the musician had a publishing deal to write music. She worked as a staff writer for a music company. This meant she wrote music for other singers.

NEW EXPERIENCE

At age 22, Maren decided to move to Tennessee. "I didn't move to Nashville with any inkling or dreams of getting a record deal," she told the *New York Times*. "I just wanted to take a break, relax, and figure out songwriting."

Maren knew Kacey well from their years performing in Texas. Kacey played a big role in getting Maren to move to Nashville too. Maren even slept on her couch for a while.

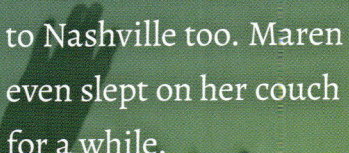

WRITING THE HITS

Soon, Kacey was turning out country music hits. Her songs were being performed by big stars like Miranda Lambert and Martina McBride. She cowrote Lambert's hit song "Mama's Broken Heart." It came out in 2013 and hit number 20 on Billboard's Hot 100 chart. The song did even better on the country music charts, hitting number two.

MUSIC ROW

Music Row is a neighborhood in Nashville, Tennessee. Many people in the music business work there. Songwriters, producers, and record labels all have offices in the area. At first, it was full of music studios. These were where artists recorded gospel and country songs. Often, "Music Row" means more than just the neighborhood. People use it to refer to the music business in Nashville more generally.

NEW CHALLENGE

Maren was also excited to try her hand at writing on "Music Row." This is an area where many musicians and producers work. The star told the *Dallas Observer*, "I wanted to become a better songwriter, so it seemed like a no-brainer to move to Nashville, where some of the best writers in the world live." Like Kacey, Maren found that she loved the work. She had spent ten years singing in small gigs around Texas. It was nice to have a different job.

MERCURY NASHVILLE

While writing music, Kacey had still been performing. She sang at open mic nights in cafés and bars around the city. Anyone can participate on these nights. It was a good chance for her to try out new material.

Kacey's hard work got her noticed. In 2012, the record label Mercury Nashville signed her. Later that year, her debut single "Merry Go 'Round" came out. It won a Grammy Award for Best Country Song of 2013.

BIG YELLOW DOG

The music publishing company Big Yellow Dog hired Maren in 2013. She worked as a songwriter. They paired her with other writers. Soon, she was writing songs for musicians like Tim McGraw and Kelly Clarkson. Then Maren had another chance to sing karaoke. It was at the company's holiday party. Her song choice was Beyoncé's "Halo." Coworkers thought her voice was amazing.

Charles Kelley

ON TOUR

The same year Kasey signed with Mercury Nashville, she had another exciting opportunity. The group Lady Antebellum invited her to go on tour. She would get to perform with them around Europe. For the band, it was a chance to help out a new artist. "We know what a big opportunity it is for a new artist to be able to go tour overseas. We're excited to take Kacey with us!" a member of the group said.

A NEW OPPORTUNITY

Maren had written some hits. However, there was a new problem. Her songwriting was becoming too personal. Other artists didn't think the songs fit them. By then, people at her company knew how well she could sing. Like Kacey, she received encouragement. They told her to try to make it as an artist. It was time to start singing the music she had been writing.

SAME TRAILER DIFFERENT PARK

Kacey's debut studio album, *Same Trailer Different Park*, came out in 2013. The artist cowrote and co-produced all the songs. Many musicians aren't as involved in their albums. When the album came out, it sounded like country music. Many of the topics were different, though. This created some controversy. For example, Kacey sang about LGBTQ rights. She also mentioned drug use. These issues were considered too modern for country. A few songs were critical of small-town life. Even though some people didn't like it, the album did well. It won Best Country Album at the 2013 Grammy Awards.

MAREN'S MUSIC ON REALITY TV

Maren had been rejected from several music competition shows. She didn't let those setbacks stop her. Once her songs became hits, contestants on those shows started to perform them. On the 15th season of *American Idol*, a contestant sang "My Church." Three different singers performed it on *The Voice* as well. Even though Maren had been turned down by those shows, she felt like she had made it when she heard her song.

"MY CHURCH"

Maren recorded a few songs for fun. In 2015, the single "My Church" came out. She had decided to release it on her own. A friend helped her get it on the platform Spotify. The track was a hit. It was streamed more than 2.5 million times in just over a month. Radio producers started to pay attention. They put the song on the air. That song "basically kick-started my entire career," Maren told the *Dallas Observer*.

STRUGGLE TO BE HEARD

Kacey had some early success. She still wasn't getting her songs played on the radio, though. Many thought her music wasn't traditional enough. The singer was frustrated. "Why wouldn't a music genre that reflects real stories not move with the times?" she wondered in an interview with *Vanity Fair*. It was hard to make it on the radio as a female artist. Country music stations play more music by men than women. In 2018, only around 11 percent of songs played were by women.

SONY MUSIC NASHVILLE

Maren had more luck getting on the radio than Kacey. This helped her career. The popularity of "My Church" was too much to ignore. Having the right connections early on also helped. Before she got a record deal, her first album was almost ready to go. That gave her more power when talking to labels. Her attitude was, "This is me. This is what I sound like. I'll release it on my own if I have to," she told *Glamour*. Sony Music Nashville wanted to sign her. They released her first full-length album, *Hero*, in 2016. It reached number one on the Billboard Top Country Albums chart.

CAREER MILESTONES

2012
Kacey's hit single "Merry Go 'Round" is released.

2013
Kacey's debut album *Same Trailer Different Park* comes out.

2014
Same Trailer Different Park wins Album of the Year at the Academy of Country Music Awards.

2015
Maren releases the extended play album *Maren Morris*.

2016
Maren's first major studio album, *Hero*, is released. She also wins a Grammy Award for Best Country Solo Performance with "My Church."

2018
Kacey releases her fourth studio album, *Golden Hour*.

2018
Maren's hit song "The Middle" reaches number five on the Billboard Hot 100.

2019
Kacey wins four Grammy Awards.

2019
Maren's album *Girl* comes out.

CHAPTER 4

STARDOM

NEW ARTIST OF THE YEAR

Kacey's music was slow to get picked up by the radio. This didn't stop her from winning awards. At the 2013 Country Music Association Awards (CMAs), she was named New Artist of the Year. The next year, "Follow Your Arrow" won the Song of the Year CMA. This was from her first studio album. It was also number two on *Billboard* magazine's 20 Best Songs of 2013 list.

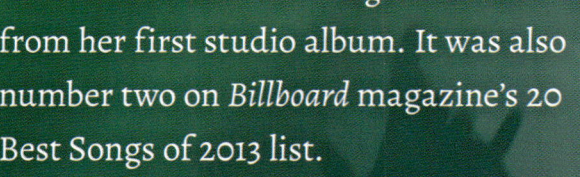

COLLECTING AWARDS

Maren began winning awards too. In 2016, she won the CMA for New Artist of the Year, just like Kacey had. The next year, Music Biz gave her a Breakthrough Artist Award. Previous winners included Sam Hunt, John Legend, and Nicki Minaj. "My Church" continued to be a hit. Maren won her first Grammy for the song. She took home Best Country Solo Performance in 2016.

PAGEANT MATERIAL

Kacey's second studio album came out in 2015. *Pageant Material* hit number one on the Country Albums list when it was released. On the record, she sang about making it as a musician. A line from the title song goes, "I'd rather lose for what I am than win for what I ain't." The singer wanted to prove that she could make it as an artist. At the same time, she didn't want to change her music or who she was just to please others.

Michael Trewartha

Zedd

Kyle Trewartha

"THE MIDDLE"

In 2018, Maren took a risk with the song "The Middle." It wasn't her typical style of music. Dance music producer Zedd had invited her to sing. The electronic music duo Grey joined her. "I am so glad that I did it, because it changed so many things for me in and out of my career," she told *Billboard*. The song was a big success. On the Pop Songs airplay list, it hit number one. Maren was only the sixth artist ever to hit number one on music lists in two different genres.

RUSTON KELLY

Kacey was at the Bluebird Café in Nashville. This is a small music club. A man started to play his guitar and sing. His back was to Kacey. Right away, she loved what she heard. "[He] played his first song, and I was just stunned by everything in it—the words, the melody, what he was saying," Kacey told *People*. The man was singer-songwriter Ruston Kelly. They began dating. In 2017, a year after hearing him sing for the first time, Kacey married Ruston.

BLUEBIRD CAFÉ

The Bluebird Café is a small music club in Nashville. It can seat 90 people for shows. Over the years, many country stars have played there. Singers and songwriters use the club to test out new songs. Shows are either "in the round" or "in the row." For "in the round" shows, musicians play in the center of the room. Listeners surround them. Musicians sing together, talk to the audience, and tell stories. "In the row" is a more traditional show. Artists perform on a small stage.

SONGWRITING PARTNER

In 2013, Maren met songwriter Ryan Hurd. They were working on a song for Tim McGraw. It was called "My Last Turn Home." The pair became friends. Later, they started dating. "I really trust his opinion, especially if I have a new song that maybe we didn't write together," Maren told *Country Living*. Ryan wrote two songs about her. One is called "Diamonds or Twine." When he asked Maren to marry him in 2017, he played this for her. The couple married in 2018.

Ryan Hurd

MORE TOURING

In 2018, Kacey went on more tours. Early in the year, she opened for the popular country group Little Big Town. That summer, Harry Styles from One Direction was touring the U.S. Kacey opened for him. While performing in New York, they surprised the crowd. The two sang a duet. It was the Shania Twain song "You're Still the One." Later that year, Kacey went on tour to promote her album *Golden Hour*.

TOURING

Touring is an important part of making it as an artist. When singers are first starting out, they often open for bigger stars. This means they perform earlier in the show. Most fans buy tickets to see the headliners. These are the main stars of the show. Opening for a bigger star is a good way for new singers to be introduced to fans.

Artists often travel on tour buses. These have lots of amenities. There is comfortable furniture for relaxing or sleeping. Some have big TVs or even recording equipment. Stars like to travel in style.

LISTENING PARTIES

Maren had also been on the road. She toured with country singers Keith Urban and Sam Hunt. Like Kacey, she opened for another former member of One Direction, Niall Horan, in 2017.

In 2018, the singer found another way to connect with fans. She hosted listening parties. Fans heard the new album *Girl* before it was released. Parties were in Nashville, Dallas, and London. Maren got the idea from Taylor Swift and Halsey.

Keith Urban

GOLDEN HOUR

Kacey released her third album, *Golden Hour*, in 2018. She wrote most of the songs after meeting her husband. The themes were new for her. More of the songs were about love. Their tone was serious. Her style was less humorous than in some earlier work. The album was recorded in Sheryl Crow's studio at her Nashville home. On writing breaks, Kacey rode horses around the property. "I never had a studio experience that was so compounded with nature," she said to *Stereogum*.

Sheryl Crow

GIRL

Maren's second album, *Girl*, came out in early 2019. It quickly reached number four on the Billboard 200. The artist was influenced by her relationship with her husband. Her first album was "very much about independence," she told *Vanity Fair*. Like Kacey, Maren then turned to writing more love songs. She also explored new styles. *Girl* isn't just a country album. It has many R&B and pop influences. "You don't have to be just one color," Maren told *Time*. "You can be a whole spectrum of things."

OH, WHAT A WORLD

In 2018, Kacey had several TV appearances. She sang on *The Late Show with Stephen Colbert*. *Saturday Night Live (SNL)* had her as the musical guest in May. The star performed two songs from *Golden Hour*. Kacey also had a small appearance in the film *Wild Rose*. Her success kept growing. Later in 2018, she launched her Oh, What a World Tour. It went to cities across the U.S. as well as to Europe. The tour continued into 2019.

TOP BILLBOARD HOT 100 SINGLES

KACEY MUSGRAVES

#60	Merry Go 'Round	9/2012
#63	Follow Your Arrow	10/2013
#98	Rainbow	2/2019

GIRL: THE WORLD TOUR

Like Kacey, Maren had performed on TV. In 2016, she was the musical guest on *SNL*. The TV show *NCIS: New Orleans* also hired her for a small role.

In 2019, Maren went on tour to promote her new album. Girl: The World Tour had dates in Mexico, Europe, Australia, and North America.

● **MAREN MORRIS**

#50	My Church	1/2016
#5	The Middle featuring Zedd, Grey	1/2018
#44	Girl	3/2019

CHAPTER 5

INFLUENCES AND COLLABORATIONS

MODERN OR TRADITIONAL?

Kacey's music is unique in the modern country music scene. Many consider her lyrics progressive. They don't always follow the typical themes found in this genre. She still uses elements of traditional country music though. Her songs are neo-traditional country with pop melodies. Like Maren, she sometimes blurs the line between country and pop. Kacey's music is considered more traditional country than Maren's.

COUNTRY OR POP?

Maren's music often mixes country and pop. Hits like "The Middle" show her pop side. "I've always had an ear for melodies, and they veer pop," she explained to the *New York Times*. "My lyrics are more country—what I love is the storytelling," she added. Many have noticed her straightforward singing style. She has been compared to Kacey in this way. Some compare her to country singers Sam Hunt and Kelsea Ballerini too.

TRADITIONAL COUNTRY

Many of Kacey's musical inspirations are traditional country artists. "I really love the old stuff. But I also respect when someone can forge a new path," she told *The Independent*. One major inspiration is country superstar Dolly Parton. Kacey called Dolly the "queen of sparkle and intelligent lyrics." *Golden Hour* was influenced by Dolly's music. The album also had non-country influences. Disco music from the 1970s was one. Another was the singer Sade.

LORETTA LYNN

Loretta Lynn is a country music singer and songwriter. She was born in 1932. Her father was a coal miner. The family didn't have much money.

She released her first single, "I'm a Honky Tonk Girl," in 1960. Around the same time, Lynn moved to Nashville. Her most famous song, "Coal Miner's Daughter," was released in 1970. It was a number-one hit. Some of her later songs were about more controversial topics. Kacey has said this is one reason she looks up to Lynn.

HARD COUNTRY

Genres like rock and hip-hop have been an inspiration to Maren. The star is also a fan of hard country music. This type of country has lyrics about difficult times in life. One example is the singer Loretta Lynn. She is an inspiration to Maren and Kacey.

Maren has some traditional country influences too. One of her favorite artists is LeAnn Rimes. "I was obsessed with [her] as a kid. I really looked up to her because she was only a few years older than me," she told the *Dallas Observer*.

Loretta Lynn

BIG STARS

Kacey's first collaborations were with songwriters. She wrote many songs for her first album with Luke Laird, Josh Osborne, and Shane McAnally. Later, she got to sing with some of her heroes. In 2014, Kacey did a duet with Loretta Lynn at the CMA Awards. The pair sang "You're Lookin' at Country." The next year, Willie Nelson recorded a duet with Kacey. They sang Nelson's song "Are You Sure."

WORKING TOGETHER

Maren has also collaborated with many artists. In 2016, she recorded the song "Dear Hate" with Vince Gill. This was in response to an act of violence at a concert. The collaboration Maren is most known for is "The Middle," with Zedd and Grey. In 2019, the artist had a chance to work with one of her idols. She and Miranda Lambert recorded "Way Too Pretty for Prison."

MIRANDA LAMBERT

Miranda Lambert is a modern country artist. Both Kacey and Maren have said her work has influenced theirs. Lambert grew up not far from where Kacey did. They studied with the same guitar teacher.

One of her earliest performances was in Johnnie High's Country Music Revue in Arlington. Maren had also performed there when she was 11 years old.

Lambert and Kacey both competed on *Nashville Star* on different seasons. Neither artist won. Kacey cowrote one of Lambert's big hits, "Mama's Broken Heart." It came out in 2013.

INSPIRATION

The two artists have many of the same influences. They share similar music backgrounds too. "Maren and I grew up singing around a lot of the same places down in Texas," Kacey told Wide Open Country. "I came to know her early on as the tiny girl with the huge voice." Kacey has also been an inspiration to Maren. She pushed boundaries in her own music. This opened the door for others to follow in her footsteps.

MUSICAL THEMES

Maren's and Kacey's songs share many similar themes. Their early records were about independence and freedom. Both later turned to love songs. The two even traveled to France together. They performed at a small country music festival. Maren learned a lot from her friend. She told *Billboard*, "Kacey inspired me to keep my strength when I went into radio tour—be kind, but be a powerful presence no one can [mess] with."

TO JUNE

Kacey has always enjoyed writing with her husband, Ruston. She told *Billboard* that when they worked together, "Songs just immediately started pouring out." In 2018, the two had the chance to perform together as well. Ruston had found a short poem written by country legend Johnny Cash. The star had written it for his wife June. Kacey's husband turned the poem into a song. He and Kacey made a recording of "To June This Morning."

THE HIGHWOMEN

In 2019, Maren joined a country music supergroup. It's called The Highwomen. Brandi Carlile, Natalie Hemby, and Amanda Shires are also in the group. Their name was based on a group from the 1980s, the Highwaymen. After working in the studio, the group did some live performances. Sheryl Crow even joined them at a festival. She had been an inspiration to Maren. "I just thought it was so cool that she was the songwriter and played bass guitar and had one of the most original voices I'd ever heard," Maren told *HuffPost*.

WILLIE NELSON
SHARED INFLUENCE

Country music legend Willie Nelson has inspired both Kacey and Maren. Many of Nelson's songs fit into the outlaw country subgenre. Some of Kacey's music does too. Here are more details about the best-selling artist and outlaw country.

Biography

- Born in 1933
- Started writing music at a young age
- Moved to Nashville in 1960 and signed his first record deal a year later
- Moved to Austin in 1972
- Performed a duet with Kacey in 2015
- Maren opened for him and sang with him in 2017

Outlaw Country

- Mixes traditional country sounds with rock influences
- Popular in the 1970s and 1980s
- Themes of being an outlaw or outsider

Famous Songs

- "Crazy" (made famous by Patsy Cline in 1961)
- "Hello Walls" (1962)
- "Blue Eyes Crying in the Rain" (1975)
- "Georgia on My Mind" (1978)

Willie Nelson

GIRL FROM GOLDEN

From Golden to Nashville, the road wasn't always easy for Kacey. The traditional country music scene didn't like her progressive lyrics. They questioned her place in country music. Getting on the radio was hard work. Still, Kacey found many fans who loved her mix of traditional and modern elements. "I'd rather have smaller numbers [of fans] that are really into what I'm doing than a massive amount of people that don't really know what I'm about," Kacey told *The Fader*.

ARTIST FROM ARLINGTON

Maren faced some of the same criticisms as Kacey. People thought her music had too many pop and rock influences. Some didn't think she was a country artist at all. She didn't let the negative comments bother her. "I'm a little bit of everything" she told *Billboard*.

CONNECTED LIVES

Both artists continue to make the music they want to make. They have shown their independence as they broke records and pushed boundaries. Maren and Kacey have shared their unique talents with the world.

TAKE A LOOK INSIDE

KANE BROWN

TWO EXTRAORDINARY PEOPLE.

SAM HUNT

CHAPTER 1

EARLY LIFE

WHO IS KANE BROWN?

Kane Brown is a social media star and country singer. He was born on October 21, 1993, in Chattanooga, Tennessee. His mother is Tabatha Brown. She raised him on her own. Growing up, Kane didn't know his father. Moving around was normal to Kane as a child. The small family lived in several different towns in Georgia and Tennessee. For a while, they lived on a farm. It belonged to Kane's grandfather.

WHO IS SAM HUNT?

Sam Hunt was born on December 8, 1984, in Cedartown, Georgia. He is a country music singer and songwriter. His parents, Joan and Allen, raised him. Joan was a third-grade teacher. Allen worked as an insurance agent. Ben and Van are Sam's younger brothers. Sam spent his whole childhood in the same town. This was very different from Kane's experience.

4

5

POWER OF A CONCERT

Kane liked R&B. He loved the way Usher sang. However, the star's songs were too high-pitched for him. The deeper notes of country songs were a better fit for his baritone voice.

A friend bought tickets to a Brad Paisley and Chris Young concert. This was the first concert Kane went to. Seeing the stars perform was a turning point, he told the *Tennessean*. That's when an idea popped into his head. He thought, "I want to do this."

ON TO NASHVILLE

Writing music hadn't seemed like a job to Sam before. It was something he enjoyed as a hobby. Then he learned that Nashville was full of music publishers and producers. They worked with songwriters. Many had written hits that Sam had heard on the radio. Moving to Nashville was the next step. "I thought that I could have a career in music," he told AL.com. "I really didn't know exactly what I wanted to do or how I would go about doing it."

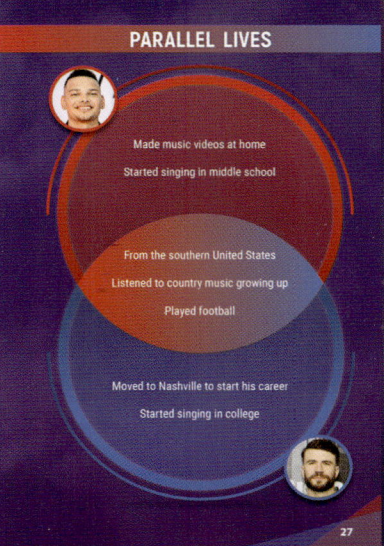

PARALLEL LIVES

Made music videos at home

Started singing in middle school

From the southern United States

Listened to country music growing up

Played football

Moved to Nashville to start his career

Started singing in college

TOP OF THE CHARTS

In October 2017, Kane set a new record. He became the first artist to top five country music charts at the same time. His music reached number one on Top Country Albums, Hot Country Songs, Country Airplay, Country Digital Song Sales, and Country Streaming Songs. Sam Hunt's "Body Like a Back Road" had been number one on the Hot Country Songs list. "What Ifs" bumped it down to number two.

TOP ALBUM

Montevallo was a success. It sold 70,000 copies in the first week. A year later, it was nominated for a Grammy Award. Like Kane, Sam also set records. He was the second male artist to lead both Top Country Albums and Hot Country Songs with his first album. Billy Ray Cyrus was the first, 22 years earlier.

TOP BILLBOARD HOT 100 SINGLES

● KANE BROWN

#82		Used to Love You Sober	10/2015
#26		What Ifs featuring Lauren Alaina	5/2017
#15		Heaven	11/2017
#28		Lose It	6/2018

● SAM HUNT

#30		Leave the Night On	6/2014
#29		Break Up in a Small Town	9/2015
#45		Make You Miss Me	3/2016
#6		Body Like a Back Road	2/2017

FOR MORE TITLES AND INFORMATION ⟶

CONNECTED LIVES™

ARIANA GRANDE
TWO EXTRAORDINARY PEOPLE.
CAMILA CABELLO

9781680217957

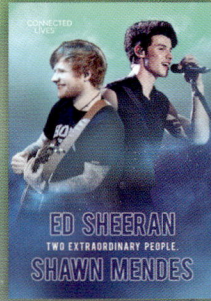

ED SHEERAN
TWO EXTRAORDINARY PEOPLE.
SHAWN MENDES

9781680217896

HALSEY
TWO EXTRAORDINARY PEOPLE.
BILLIE EILISH

9781680217919

JOHN LEGEND
TWO EXTRAORDINARY PEOPLE.
MICHAEL BUBLÉ

9781680217926

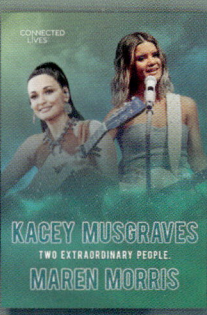

KACEY MUSGRAVES
TWO EXTRAORDINARY PEOPLE.
MAREN MORRIS

9781680217964

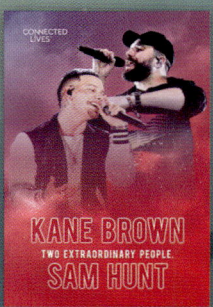

KANE BROWN
TWO EXTRAORDINARY PEOPLE.
SAM HUNT

9781680217902

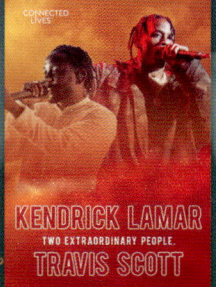

KENDRICK LAMAR
TWO EXTRAORDINARY PEOPLE.
TRAVIS SCOTT

9781680217933

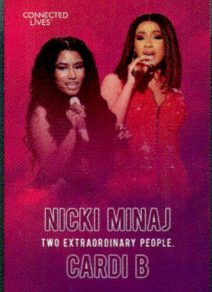

NICKI MINAJ
TWO EXTRAORDINARY PEOPLE.
CARDI B

9781680217940

MORE TITLES COMING SOON
SDLBACK.COM/CONNECTED-LIVES